The River

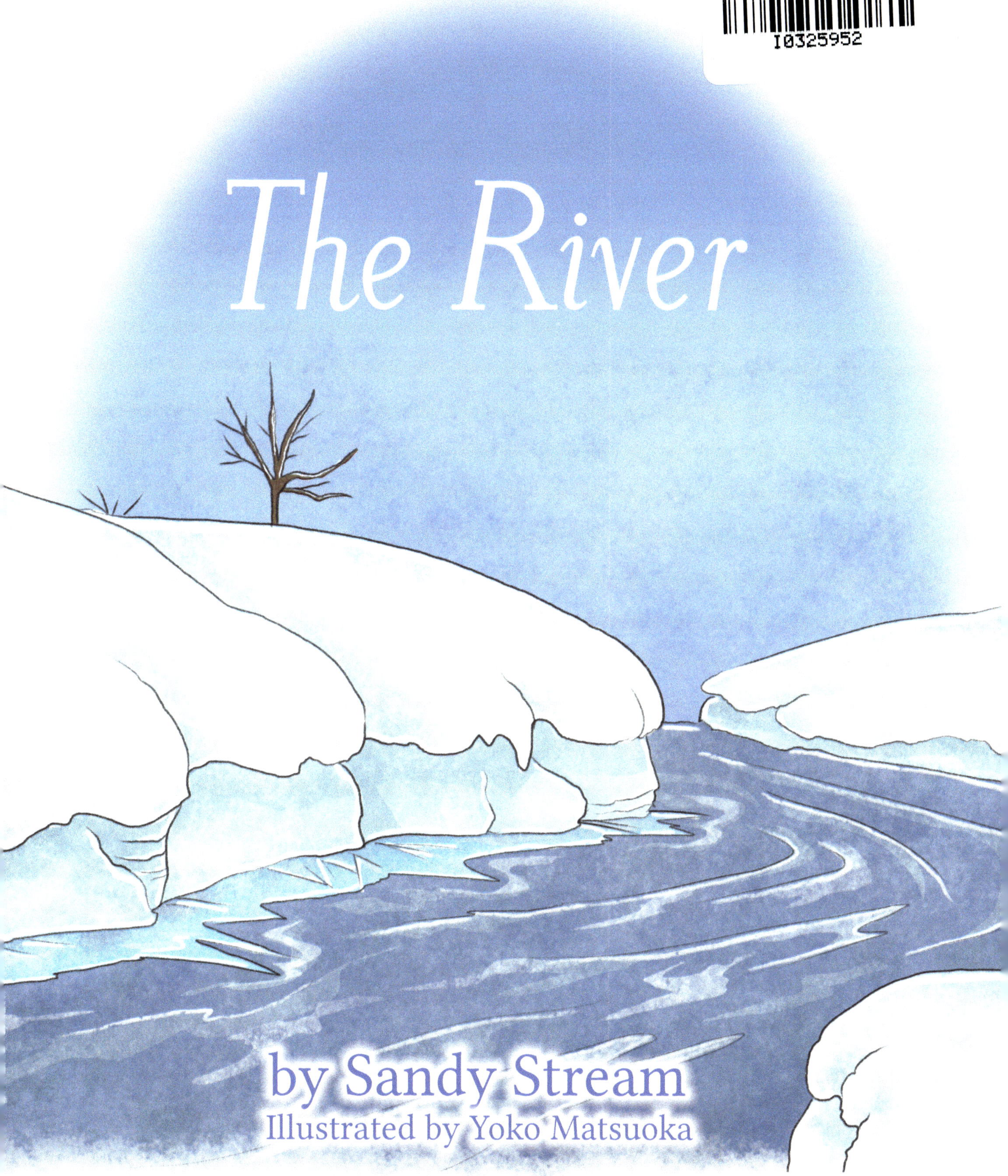

by Sandy Stream
Illustrated by Yoko Matsuoka

The River. By Sandy Stream
Illustrated by Yoko Matsuoka
Edited by Tomoko Matsuoka

ISBN 978-0-9739481-5-8

Copyright © 2014 by Sandy Stream Publishing. Montreal, Canada.
All rights reserved. No part of this book may be reproduced, stored in a retrieval system, or transmitted in any form or by any means without the written permission of Sandy Stream Publishing.

On a Personal Note

Our bodies are made up of more than 70 percent water. If we observe the rivers outside, we can learn a tremendous amount about our rivers inside.

Sandy Stream

Based on the truth of nature

There was once a river
and the river flowed.

Many animals came and drank from the river.

In the winter, snow fell on the river and froze the river's edges.

The river continued to flow without any resistance.

One spring day, children came and threw some rocks into the river.

The river flowed around the rocks. She always moved; she never stopped flowing.

One summer day, a young bird sat near the river and poured water into the river.

The river absorbed the tears and continued to flow without any attempt to change anything.

In the fall, a mama bird visited the cave near the river many times. One day, she squawked and shook the cave so hard that it caused ripples in the river.

The river felt the ripples and continued to flow without any thought.

Then there was a storm in the cave near the river that caused huge waves.

The river rose with the storm and continued to flow without any attempt to control anything. The river settled after the storm.

The next day, a dark cloud passed over the river...

The river continued to flow in its shadow, knowing that the darkness would pass.

The river brought some of her waters to the vast ocean where they were welcomed and absorbed…and continued to flow without any concern for the next moment.

The always

The River Series

Sparky Can Fly
Sparky's Mama
Tweets and Hurricanes
Feathers
Flex
Roots
The River

www.RiverSpeaks.com

www.ingramcontent.com/pod-product-compliance
Lightning Source LLC
Chambersburg PA
CBHW061121010526
44112CB00024B/2942